The Easter Story

From the Gospels of Matthew, Mark, Luke, and John

Illustrated by

Cathy Ann Johnson

Tommy
NELSON

Thomas Nelson, Inc.
Nashville

A great crowd in Jerusalem heard that Jesus was coming there. . . . They took branches of palm trees and went out to meet Jesus. They shouted,

"Praise God!
God bless the One who comes in the name of the Lord!
God bless the King of Israel!"

The Pharisees said to each other, "You can see that nothing is going right for us. Look! The whole world is following him."

Jesus entered Jerusalem and went into the Temple.

The leading priests and the teachers of the law. . .began trying to find a way to kill Jesus. They were afraid of him because all the people were amazed at his teaching.

JOHN 12: 12–13, 19; MARK 11: 11, 18

On the first day of the Feast of Unleavened Bread, . . . Jesus was sitting at the table with his 12 followers. . . . Then Jesus said, ". . . One of you 12 will turn against me." This made the followers very sad.

Then Judas said to Jesus, "Teacher, surely I am not the one. Am I?" . . .

Jesus answered, "Yes, it is you."

While they were eating, Jesus took some bread. He thanked God for it and broke it. Then he gave it to his followers and said, "Take it. This bread is my body." Then Jesus took a cup. He thanked God for it and gave it to the followers. . . . Then Jesus said, "This is my blood which begins the new agreement that God makes with his people."

MATTHEW 26: 17, 20–22, 25; MARK 14: 22–24

Jesus told the followers, "Tonight you will lose your faith because of me. . . ."

Peter said, "All the other followers may lose their faith because of you. But I will never lose my faith."

Jesus said, ". . . Tonight you will say you don't know me . . . three times before the rooster crows."

But Peter said, "I will never say that I don't know you! I will even die with you!"

MATTHEW 26: 31–35

Jesus and his followers went to a place called Gethsemane. He said to his followers, "Sit here while I pray."

Jesus told Peter, James, and John to come with him. . . . He said to them, ". . . Stay here and watch." Jesus walked a little farther. . . . Then he fell on the ground and prayed.

"My Father, if it is not possible for this painful thing to be taken from me, and if I must do it, then I pray that what you want will be done."

Then Jesus went back to the followers and said, "You are . . . sleeping . . . ? Get up. We must go. Here comes the man who has turned against me."

MARK 14: 32–35; MATTHEW 26: 42, 45–46

While Jesus was still speaking, Judas came up. . . . He had many people with him. They had been sent from the leading priests and the older leaders of the people. They carried swords and clubs. Judas had planned to give them a signal. He had said, "The man I kiss is Jesus. Arrest him." At once Judas went to Jesus and . . . kissed him.

Then the men came and grabbed Jesus and arrested him. . . . All of Jesus' followers left him and ran away.

Those men who arrested Jesus led him to the house of Caiaphas, the high priest. . . . Peter followed Jesus but did not go near him.

MATTHEW 26: 47–58

Peter was sitting in the courtyard. A servant girl came to him and said, "You were with Jesus. . . ."

But Peter said that he was never with Jesus. . . . At the gate, another girl saw him. . . . Again, Peter said that he was never with Jesus. . . . Later, some people . . . said, "We know you are one of those men who followed Jesus. . . ."

[Peter] said, " . . . I don't know the man." After Peter said this, a rooster crowed. Then he remembered what Jesus had told him: "Before the rooster crows, you will say three times that you don't know me." Then Peter went outside and cried.

MATTHEW 26: 69–75

Early the next morning, all the leading priests and older leaders of the people decided to kill Jesus. They tied him, led him away, and turned him over to Pilate, the governor.

Pilate asked him, "Are you the King of the Jews?"

Jesus answered, "Yes, I am."

Every year at the time of Passover the governor would free one person from prison. This was always a person the people wanted to be set free.

Pilate said, "I have Barabbas and Jesus. Which do you want me to set free for you?"

The people answered, "Barabbas!"

Pilate asked, "What should I do with Jesus? . . ."

They all answered, "Kill him on a cross! . . . Then Pilate freed Barabbas.

MATTHEW 27: 1–2, 11, 15, 21–22, 26

Pilate's soldiers took Jesus into the governor's palace. . . .
Then the soldiers used thorny branches to make a crown.
They put this crown of thorns on Jesus' head. . . . After they
finished making fun of Jesus, . . . they led Jesus away.

The soldiers nailed Jesus to a cross. They put a sign above Jesus' head with the charge against him written on it. The sign read: "THIS IS JESUS, THE KING OF THE JEWS."

Matthew 27: 27, 29, 31, 35, 37

There were also two criminals led out with Jesus to be killed.

One of the criminals began to shout insults at Jesus. . . . But the other criminal stopped him. He said, ". . . We are punished justly; we should die. But this man has done nothing wrong!" Then this criminal said to Jesus, "Jesus, remember me when you come into your kingdom!"

Then Jesus said to him, ". . . Today you will be with me in paradise!"

LUKE 23: 32, 39–43

It was about noon, and the whole land became dark until three o'clock in the afternoon. There was no sun! The curtain in the Temple was torn into two pieces. Jesus cried out in a loud voice, "Father, I give you my life." After Jesus said this, he died.

A follower of Jesus from the town of Arimathea . . . took the body and wrapped it in a clean linen cloth. He put Jesus' body in a new tomb that he had cut in a wall of rock. He rolled a very large stone to block the entrance of the tomb.

LUKE 23: 44–46; MATTHEW 27: 57–60

Very early on the first day of the week, the women came to the tomb where Jesus' body was laid. . . . They found that the stone had been rolled away from the entrance of the tomb. They went in, but they did not find the body of the Lord Jesus. . . . Two men in shining clothes suddenly stood beside them. . . . The men said to the women, "Why are you looking for a living person here? This is a place for the dead. Jesus is not here. He has risen from death!"

The women left the tomb and told all these things to the 11 apostles and the other followers. . . . The women told the apostles everything that had happened at the tomb. But they did not believe the women.

LUKE 24: 1–6, 9–11

Later Jesus showed himself to the 11 followers while they were eating.

He said to them, "Peace be with you."

. . . They thought they were seeing a ghost. But Jesus said, ". . . Why do you doubt what you see? Look at my hands and my feet. . . . Touch me. You can see that I have a living body. . . ." After Jesus said this, he showed them his hands and feet. The followers were amazed and very happy.

MARK 16: 14; LUKE 24: 36–41

Jesus led his followers out of Jerusalem almost to
Bethany. He raised his hands and blessed them.
While he was blessing them, he was separated from
them and carried into heaven. They worshiped him
and then went back to the city very happy. They
stayed in the Temple all the time, praising God.

LUKE 24: 50–53